Hawai'i's Animals

Do the Most Amazing Things!

Marion Coste
Illustrated by Rena Ekmanis

A Latitude 20 Book

UNIVERSITY OF HAWAI'I PRESS
HONOLULU

© 2015 University of Hawai'i Press
Printed in China

20 19 18 17 16 15   6 5 4 3 2 1

Library of Congress Cataloging-in-Publication Data
Coste, Marion, author.
  Hawai'i's animals do the most amazing things! / Marion Coste and
Rena Ekmanis, illustrator.
     pages cm
  "A latitude 20 book."
  Includes bibliographical references.
  ISBN 978-0-8248-3962-8 (cloth : alk. paper)
  1. Animals—Hawaii—Juvenile literature.   I. Ekmanis, Rena, illustrator.
II. Title.
  QL345.H3C67 2014
  590.9969—dc23
                                                    2014014460

University of Hawai'i Press books are printed on acid-free
paper and meet the guidelines for permanence and
durability of the Council on Library Resources.

Designed by Mardee Melton
Printed by Regent Publishing Services

Contents

This book is dedicated to my husband, Bill,
who makes all things possible.

Hawai'i
Life in the Middle of the Sea

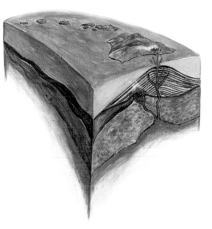

Hawai'i is different from anywhere else on earth. On a world map, it looks like a group of tiny dots in the middle of the Pacific Ocean, the biggest ocean on the planet. Looking closer, you find Hawai'i is an **archipelago**, a chain of islands, separated from other large land areas by more than two thousand miles of open ocean.

The islands are really the tips of giant mountains that rise from the bottom of the sea. They were formed when the Pacific Plate, one of the giant **tectonic plates** that make up the earth's crust, moved slowly across a "hot spot" where the hot liquid core of the earth leaks through. Over the hot spot, **magma** rose through the crust and formed an underwater volcano. Flowing **lava** slowly built the volcano higher and higher until it stood above the sea. Meanwhile, the plate moved on, carrying the volcano away from the hot spot. Lava cooled into rock, the volcano became an island, and a new volcano formed over the hot spot.

For millions of years, wind and weather wore away the islands' volcanic rock, and as the Pacific Plate moved toward the northwest, the older islands grew smaller, almost as if they were melting back into the sea. Today, the Hawaiian chain stretches over 1,500 miles of ocean, from the youngest, the Big Island of Hawai'i in the southeast, to the oldest, tiny Kure **atoll** in the northwest. Beyond Kure, underwater **seamounts** are all that remain of older islands.

The hot spot is still active. It lies under the Big Island, where lava flows down the slopes of **Kīlauea** to the sea. The hot spot is also building the future island of Lō'ihi, which is rising from the ocean floor about 18 miles off the southeast coast of the island of Hawai'i.

Animal Life Comes to the Islands

After the volcanic islands had cooled and wind and weather had turned the surface rock into soil, plants and animals began to arrive. It was very hard for living things to get to Hawai'i because the islands were so far away from other land areas. When an animal or plant did arrive, it was usually by chance.

All the living things that made it to Hawai'i traveled by wind, wing, or wave. Some seeds and tiny insects drifted to the islands on the wind. Flying animals like birds, bats, or large insects may have been blown off course while they were in the air and were carried to the islands by storms or strong winds. Other plants and tiny animals "hitchhiked" on the feathers and feet of birds (sometimes seeds arrived in bird droppings), and still others floated with the ocean currents, sometimes clinging to logs or other objects that bobbed on the surface of the sea.

Most of the animals that got to Hawai'i didn't survive. They couldn't find the foods or habitats they needed. The island environment was too different from the homes they had left. A very few managed to adapt, or adjust, to the new living conditions. They became the **progenitors** of today's native Hawaiian species.

Staying Alive

The most important goal of all animals is to survive. Everything about an animal—the way it looks and the way it acts—relates to one of three basic drives: to find food, to escape from predators, and to reproduce (have babies). When an animal can do all these things, it survives as an individual and also helps its species survive.

Animals must find habitats that provide food, protection from enemies, and safe places to breed and raise young. If an animal's habitat is changed or destroyed, and the animal can't adjust to its new surroundings, it dies.

Within a habitat, each animal has its **niche**, its special place. In a forest, for instance, there are animals that live on the ground, animals that live in bushes, and animals that live high among the trees. All the animals that live together in one area depend on each other for survival.

Learning about Animals

When we study animals, we want to know two things: how they are made (structures) and how they act (behaviors). "Structure" means more than just bones and muscles; it also means shape, size, body covering (fur, feathers, skin, or scales), and color.

Sometimes, structures and behaviors work together to help animals survive. For instance, some baby chicks in nests on the ground have colored markings (structures) that look exactly like their surroundings. When a hawk flies overhead, the chicks stay perfectly still (behavior) so that the predator can't see them.

Evolution in the Hawaiian Islands

Evolution occurs when an animal (or plant) changes in such a way that it is better able to survive in a certain habitat. In Hawai'i, as time passed, the animals and plants that had adapted to life in the islands slowly changed. Sometimes the changes were in behavior, and sometimes in body structure. Through thousands of generations and millions of years, animals passed these adaptations down to their young. Gradually, the animals and plants that had first come to Hawai'i **evolved** into new species.

As animals spread out into areas of the islands with different living conditions, and then moved from older islands to newer islands, they continued to change. Some birds developed different kinds of beaks that helped them eat different kinds of foods. The colors of some animals changed so that they were better **camouflaged**, and some animals completely changed the way they hunted and fed. Evolution is not fast. Scientists think it took about 27 million years for these changes to take place.

Native, Endemic, and Indigenous Species

The animal species that came to Hawai'i on their own before humans are called "native." Some of these native animal species, like the *nēnē,* are **endemic**, which means they live only in Hawai'i. Other natives, like the spinner dolphins, are **indigenous**, which means they live in Hawai'i and also in other places. Most of Hawai'i's native animals are endemic, found nowhere else in the world.

Human Impact

Hawai'i has few native predators. Sadly, the biggest threats to Hawai'i's native species come from humans. When people first came to Hawai'i to live, they brought new plants and animals with them. The species they brought are called introduced or **alien** species. Introduced animals and plants are often invasive, which means they spread quickly and take over food and habitats, forcing out native species.

Native Hawaiian species, both plants and animals, which had lived without predators for millions of years, had lost their ability to defend themselves. Many of these native species became **extinct** because they couldn't avoid introduced predators or **compete** with invasive species for food and living space. Today, most of Hawai'i's native plants and animals are found only high in the mountains, away from humans and alien species.

Besides bringing in plants and animals that pushed native species out of their natural habitats, humans destroyed much of Hawai'i's grasslands, wetlands, and forests in order to build farms, roads, cities, resorts, and shopping centers.

Hawai'i has lost more native species to extinction than any of our other United States. More than 70 percent of Hawai'i's native forest birds are extinct. Today, there are more endangered species per square mile on the Hawaiian Islands than in any other place on earth.

Nature's Mysteries

In spite of all the challenges, Hawai'i is home to a fascinating assortment of plants and animals, many of which are found nowhere else in the world. Researchers study these living creatures to learn how they live, breed, and defend themselves, and how they are important to Hawai'i's **ecosystems**. These scientists are uncovering new information all the time, but the world of nature still holds many mysteries.

In the following pages, you will read about some of Hawai'i's amazing animals, such as singing whales, spinning dolphins, and bats that turn somersaults in the air. Their actions seem strange to us, but in some way, these behaviors help the animals survive. Some animals in this book, like the *wēkiu* bug and the killer caterpillars, have adapted in unusual ways and evolved into animals unlike any others.

As we learn about animals and how they live, we begin to see how different parts of the natural world fit together, and how perfectly animals are designed for survival. We also become aware of how much we don't know yet, and how human activity has affected animal and plant life, not only in Hawai'i, but all over the world. The more we learn, the better we will be able to protect the spectacular natural beauty and remarkable native species of the Hawaiian Islands.

Flying Bullies

Species: Great Frigatebird
Scientific Name: *Frigata minor palmerstoni*
Hawaiian Name: 'Iwa
Category: Indigenous Native Hawaiian Species
Status: Not endangered

High above the island shoreline, big fork-tailed birds glide with the wind, turning and rising on long black wings. Far out on the horizon, other birds appear. The distant birds are brown **boobies**, flying back from a day's hunt over the open ocean. The boobies carry fish in their beaks, dinner for their chicks waiting on land.

As the boobies get closer, the big black birds dive at them and chase them until the boobies let go of the fish they are carrying. Bits of food drop through the air, and the black birds, known as great frigatebirds but called 'iwa (thief) by Hawaiians, swoop down and snap them up.

Although people think of 'iwa as flying bullies that get their dinners by stealing from other birds, they actually hunt and catch most of their food on their own. They fly far out over the open ocean, then swoop down to catch the flying fish that are skimming the waves. Sometimes they dip their heads into the water and use their hooked beaks to snag fish or squid swimming near the surface. Sometimes 'iwa join other seabirds and fly in large groups over the ocean, waiting for large predator fish such as tuna to chase schools of smaller fish up to the surface. On land, 'iwa sometimes eat the **hatchlings** of other seabirds, flying low over nests and plucking out the helpless chicks.

'Iwa are perfectly built for life in the air. When they are full-grown, their outspread wings measure more than seven feet tip to tip. These long wings enable them to soar on the wind without using much energy, opening and closing their scissor-shaped tails as they fly. 'Iwa can stay in flight for several days and nights, and may even sleep on the wing. Their feathers are not waterproof, so they cannot rest on the water.

When they are on land, frigatebirds perch in trees or bushes. They may land on the ground, but if they do, they have trouble getting back into the air because their legs are short, their feet small and weak, and their wings very long. Frigatebirds like to be in large groups when they roost. Sometimes, during the day, they sit upright and open their wings wide to sun themselves.

Male and female 'iwa look very different. The male frigatebird is all black with a glossy green-and-purple sheen on its head, neck, and upper back. It has a big red throat pouch that it can blow up like a balloon. The female is larger than the male and not as glossy on the head and neck. She has a white breast and gray throat but can't **inflate** her throat patch.

When male 'iwa look for mates, they get together in groups on the ground, blow up their throat pouches, make snapping sounds with their beaks, and wave their heads and wings at females flying above them. Each male builds a flat nest of twigs and branches in a bush or low tree. Males will often try to steal nest materials from each other, sometimes even chasing other males up into the air.

The female 'iwa lays one egg, and both parents take turns sitting on it. After fifty-one to fifty-seven days, the chick hatches. Both parents feed the chick until it learns to fly, which may take almost two months, and then the female keeps on feeding the chick for up to sixteen months. 'Iwa care for their young longer than any other bird.

Frigatebirds that have mated stay fairly close to their nesting areas, but birds that are too young to breed (less than eight to ten years old) and adults that have not mated often fly great distances over the open ocean. Some young birds that had leg bands put on them in the Northwestern Hawaiian Islands were later found in the Philippines—almost 9,000 miles away.

The 'iwa, or great frigatebird, is not an endangered species, but the number of 'iwa in the wild is getting smaller. Luckily, the Northwestern Hawaiian Islands, where the birds usually nest, have no mongooses, rats, or **feral** cats to prey on eggs and chicks. Scientists are working to keep the species plentiful by creating new breeding areas, protecting the birds from introduced predators, and limiting destruction of their habitat.

Fisher Bird

SPECIES: Black-crowned night heron
SCIENTIFIC NAME: *Nycticorax nycticorax hoactli*
HAWAIIAN NAME: *ʻAukuʻu*
CATEGORY: Indigenous Native Hawaiian Species
STATUS: Stable, not endangered

On a golf course on Kauaʻi, some golfers tossed seeds on the ground near a small pond to feed redheaded cardinals. A black-crowned night heron left the pond and came over to join the smaller birds. Instead of eating the seeds, the heron picked them up, carried them over to the pond, and dropped them in the water. The golfers watched as the heron stood absolutely still on the shore and waited until some small fish swam to the seeds, then—quick as a flash—the heron grabbed the fish and gobbled them down. The golfers were amazed. A bird was using the seeds as bait to catch its dinner!

Over the next few months, the golfers threw out bread and watched the heron run down to the water or flick its head sideways to toss the bread into the pond, then place the bread so it would attract fish. If a large Japanese *koi*, too big for the heron to eat, went after the bread, the heron lifted the bread out of the water until the big fish swam away. Then the bird replaced the bread and waited until the right-sized fish came along.

News of the fishing heron spread, and soon reports came in from other people who had seen the same thing. Near a restaurant on the leeward side of Oʻahu, a heron in a group of black swans grabbed a piece of bread, took it to the water, and pushed it down into the water again and again until it caught a fish. Within ten minutes it had caught four fish.

Scientists used to think only humans used tools. As researchers studied animal behaviors more closely, however, they began to realize that other animals were using simple tools. For example, chimpanzees poke sticks into ant or termite hills to draw out the insects, and sea otters use rocks to crack open shellfish. A few birds have also been seen using tools, including herons, but it was not until 2007 that Hawai'i's only **resident** heron, the black-crowned night heron, was seen using a tool—seeds—to catch fish.

Black-crowned night herons, *'auku'u* in Hawaiian, are found everywhere in the world except Australia and Antarctica. They are the only herons native to Hawai'i and are found on all the main islands near any kind of water, including mountain streams, lowland ponds, fish hatcheries, concrete channels, and golf-course water hazards. Named for the dark blue-gray coloring on the top of its head, Hawai'i's herons hunt and feed during the day as well as at night. They sit so still, watching the water for prey, that people sometimes mistake them for statues. When a fish appears, the heron flashes into action, plunging its long black bill into the water and picking up a fish faster than the human eye can see.

Hawai'i's heron is a handsome bird. Males and females look alike, and during the early summer breeding season, both grow long white plumes that trail from the back of their heads.

The ʻaukuʻu prefers to hunt alone and will chase away other herons that invade its space. It catches and eats many different kinds of prey: fish, frogs, snakes, mice, insects, crayfish, and sometimes baby ducks or seabirds.

The worst threat that faces ʻaukuʻu is the loss of habitat. Very little of Hawaiʻi's original **wetlands** remain, and every year, more wetlands are drained, filled, paved, or polluted. Scientists are trying to establish areas called **sanctuaries** where birds can live safely, and they are working on a plan to protect and restore Hawaiʻi's wetlands.

Other threats to herons include introduced animals such as dogs, rats, feral cats, mongooses, cattle egrets, and barn owls. Sometimes introduced plants such as **water hyacinths** clog waterways and reduce the amount of open water herons need for hunting. The disease called **botulism** threatens all of Hawaiʻi's waterbirds, as do fuel and oil spills that **contaminate** island waters. In spite of these threats, the number of Hawaiʻi's black-crowned night herons seems to be holding steady, and they are not an endangered species.

Bird with No Nest

SPECIES: Fairy tern (white tern)
SCIENTIFIC NAME: *Gygis alba*
HAWAIIAN NAME: *Manu-o-Kū*
CATEGORY: Indigenous Native Hawaiian Species
STATUS: Threatened

Fairy terns have a risky way of taking care of their eggs. Instead of gathering twigs or grasses to build a nest, the small female seabird finds a fork in a tree or a small scar on a branch and lays her egg there. If trees are scarce, she'll put her egg in a low bush, on a rock ledge, a piece of coral, or even a building.

You would think the egg would roll off and break. Incredibly, it doesn't. Scientists who study the terns found three reasons for this. First, before it lays its egg, the tern "trims" a knothole or scar in a tree with the side of its claw to make it better for holding an egg. Second, the oval shape of the egg, rounded at both ends, keeps it from rolling. Third, the parents take turns guarding the egg around the clock, holding it firmly in place with their chest feathers.

After the female lays one speckled egg, she and her mate take care of it for about a month. If something should happen to the egg, the female will lay a second one. Most fairy terns lay their eggs in May or June and take care of their chicks until sometime in September. Then the birds fly out to sea until the next breeding season.

The official name of the fairy tern is "white tern." Hawaiians call it *manu-o-Kū,* and some people call it the "love tern." It has pure white feathers and big blue eyes ringed with black, and it darts and dips gracefully in flight, like a fairy might. It seems to have no fear of people and sometimes hovers in the air over people's heads.

Fairy terns are seabirds and spend most of their time out over the ocean except when they breed. They are native to Hawai'i and indigenous, which means they are found in other places besides the Hawaiian islands, such as the South Pacific, Indian, and South Atlantic Oceans.

In Hawai'i, the terns breed on many of the Northwestern Hawaiian Islands, but only on O'ahu in the main islands. They can be spotted at Kapi'olani Park and Fort DeRussy in Waikīkī, and in the downtown Honolulu area near 'Iolani Palace. In the city, fairy terns like to lay their eggs in large trees such as the banyan, *kukui,* and monkeypod. Surprisingly, the "city chicks" on O'ahu have a higher survival rate than the "country chicks" in the Northwestern Hawaiian Islands. Perhaps better egg-balancing spots in the large trees of the main islands help the chicks survive.

When the chicks hatch, they cling to their branch or ledge with strong, sharp claws. They are very good at holding on, even during high winds. Both parents feed the chicks, taking turns flying out over the ocean to catch fish. When they hunt, the terns dive down to the surface of the sea and catch small, shiny fish, mostly young goatfish, flying fish, and squid. They carry the fish crosswise in their sharp black bills and feed them one at a time to their chicks. The chicks swallow the fish headfirst.

When the chicks are about seven weeks old, they can fly. They make short flights around the breeding site. In another two weeks, they begin to fish for themselves. Once the young terns can feed themselves, they live at sea. They hunt alone or in mixed flocks with other kinds of seabirds, feeding on small fish chased to the surface by large predator fish such as tuna or sharks. In three to five years, fairy terns are old enough to breed. Then they return to land.

In ancient times, fairy terns were sacred to the Hawaiians. Navigators would watch the flight of the terns to find land. If the sailors saw the birds flying in the morning, they would sail in the direction from which the birds came. If they saw the terns in the evening, the sailors could follow them to land. One navigator says he believes fairy terns are able to fly as far as 120 miles offshore.

Fairy terns are plentiful on the Northwestern Hawaiian Islands, and their number on Oʻahu has increased from one nesting pair in 1961 to 250 pairs in 2005. The major threats to them on Oʻahu come from rats and feral cats. On the island of Midway in the Northwestern Hawaiian Islands, big-headed ants have been seen attacking eggs as they hatch and even adult birds that are sitting on the eggs. Overfishing of large fish such as ʻahi (tuna) may affect the eating habits of the terns because they depend on the predator fish to drive smaller fish toward the surface. Scientists are keeping track of the tern population to see if this species or its habitats need protection.

Snail Bird Bath

NAME: ʻElepaio
SCIENTIFIC NAME: *Chasiempis sandwichensis*
HAWAIIAN NAME: *ʻElepaio*
CATEGORY: Endemic Native Hawaiian Species
STATUS: Endangered on the island of Oʻahu

One of the strangest of all bird behaviors is called "anting." When a birds "ants," it picks up ants or other objects and rubs them over its body and wings, kind of like taking a bath. Many species of birds have been seen anting using different creatures, including ants, beetles, wasps, **centipedes**, and caterpillars. Some birds have used vinegar, mustard, onions, lemon peels, hair tonic, mothballs, and even smoke from chimneys or cigarettes. No matter what item or animal is used, the behavior is still called "anting."

In Hawaiʻi, the little *ʻelepaio*, a bold and curious forest bird, has been seen anting with four different things: a garlic snail, fruit from the Brazilian pepper tree, a **millipede**, and an ant. One scientist watched an *ʻelepaio* pick up a garlic snail, hold it in its bill, then wipe the snail on the underside of its wings and near the base of its tail. The bird then dropped the snail and used its bill to **preen** the feathers where it had rubbed the snail. Another time, the same scientist watched an *ʻelepaio* pick up a berry from a Christmas berry tree, wipe it on his breast, then drop the berry and preen its breast feathers.

Why does the *ʻelepaio* choose these four items? They all seem to have something special in their juice or bodily fluids. We know that the garlic snail gives off a strong odor of garlic or onions when it is disturbed. The Christmas berry tree is related to poison ivy. Its sap will cause itching and rash, and some parts of this plant have been used to treat infections. Although we don't know which species of millipede the *ʻelepaio* used, we do

17

know that some millipedes are **toxic**. If you pick one up, it has a bitter, sharp smell. Ants can give off a stinging liquid called formic acid. Is it possible the *'elepaio* is using these things as a kind of medicine?

Nobody knows exactly why birds ant. Some scientists think the birds are using the fluids from the insects or plants to soothe their skin or get rid of **parasites** such as lice or mites. There are two kinds of anting: active, where a bird will pick up the ant and rub it on its feathers; and passive, where a bird just sits on an anthill and spreads out his wings and tail, letting the ants crawl through its feathers. Anting seems to make the birds feel better in some way. Sometimes, birds that have anted seem to be a little drunk—they tremble or have trouble walking.

The *'elepaio* is a native songbird that lives in the forests of O'ahu, Hawai'i, and Kaua'i. It is very active and alert and can catch insects almost anywhere—in the air, on leaves and branches, on the ground, and by pecking them out of the bark of trees. *'Elepaio* were important to Hawaiians in ancient times. Canoe makers believed that the bird was their guardian spirit because it would follow them through the forest as they looked for strong, healthy trees. After a tree was cut down, the canoe builders watched the *'elepaio*. If the bird pecked at the fallen tree, it was known to be full of bugs and therefore not good for making a canoe. If the bird left the tree alone, the builders knew it was good for building a strong canoe.

How the *'elepaio* has learned to ant is one of nature's mysteries. Scientists think *'elepaio* existed in Hawai'i for at least 2.3 million years before people arrived. The little birds couldn't have anted then, because the islands had no native ants, and native Hawaiian plants and animals didn't have stingers, poisons, or other **chemical defenses**. Garlic snails, Christmas berry trees, millipedes, and ants were brought to the islands by humans millions of years later. How did the *'elepaio* figure out how to use these introduced species?

The *'elepaio* is one of the few native Hawaiian birds that has survived the introduction of new plants and animals, but the little songbird still faces many threats. Black rats, feral cats, and mongooses prey on *'elepaio* nests. Mosquitoes carry diseases that are deadly to the *'elepaio*. Invasive introduced plants have pushed out native plants important to the bird's survival, and the *'elepaio*'s habitat has been damaged or destroyed by feral pigs and goats, human development, and wildfires. On O'ahu, where the damage to forests has destroyed most of the bird's habitat, the *'elepaio* is an endangered species.

Two Birds in One

SPECIES: Pacific golden plover
SCIENTIFIC NAME: *Dominica fulva*
HAWAIIAN NAME: *Kōlea*
CATEGORY: Indigenous Native Hawaiian Species
STATUS: Not endangered

In Hawaiʻi, people can tell the seasons are changing by looking at birds called *kōlea*. In winter, the *kōlea*'s feathers are brown and gold, but as summer approaches, these long-legged shorebirds shed their brown colors and grow bright black-and-white feathers. The winter bird looks so different from the summer one that you might think they were two different birds.

Why do they make such a change? *Kōlea*, also called Pacific golden plovers, spend the winter in Hawaiʻi. They can be found on all the islands, hunting for food in low grassy areas. Their brown-and-gold winter **plumage** helps them blend into their background and makes them hard to see. In late spring, *kōlea* change their colors to black-and-white and leave Hawaiʻi to make the long flight over almost three thousand miles of open sea to Alaska. In the Arctic, *kōlea*'s summer colors have two purposes: to attract mates and to give them camouflage from arctic predators.

All birds depend on their feathers for life. Feathers keep them warm and help them fly. To keep their feathers in good shape, birds often preen them, running their claws or beaks through them to get rid of dust, spread out body oil, and keep the feathers in order. Even with all this attention, feathers wear out. When they do, they loosen and fall out, and new feathers push their way through to replace them. This is called **molting**. *Kōlea* molt twice every year, once in the spring when they are getting ready to go to Alaska, and once in the early fall, after they have returned to Hawai'i.

The unusual thing about the *kōlea*'s molt is that the new feathers look so different from the feathers that have been shed. Winter *kōlea* are gray and brown with golden flecks on their backs and white to pale yellow underneath. Males and females look alike, and the young are colored the same way. The birds are very hard to see when they stand in the grass. During winter days in Hawai'i, *kōlea* spend their time hunting for food, resting, and keeping intruders out of their territories. In the evenings, they fly to their nighttime roosts, which are often on high, flat rooftops, like the one at Kahala Mall on O'ahu. While they are in Hawai'i, *kōlea* often live near humans, sometimes even taking food from people's hands. People like to have the birds nearby because they eat insect pests.

At the end of February, *kōlea*'s feathers begin to loosen and the birds start their springtime molt. By the end of April, you can tell the females from the males: the males' bellies and faces are jet black, and a bright white band runs above their eyes and down their chests. Females have black chests too, but some light feathers speckle them.

By the first week in May, 90 percent of the *kōlea* have left Hawai'i for Alaska. A few *kōlea* don't fly north, spending the summer in Hawai'i instead. As if they knew they weren't going to need showy black-and-white plumage, the birds that stay in Hawai'i don't completely change their colors. In Alaska, the *kōlea*'s black-and-white colors form a **disruptive** pattern that breaks up the outline of the bird's body so that predators—especially flying ones—have trouble spotting the nesting bird.

The different colors that *kōlea* wear in summer and winter help the birds survive in two very different habitats. How nature knows what color feathers *kōlea* need, and when they need them, is a mystery. Scientists have learned that chemicals in the birds' bodies control the growth of new feathers, and they think changes in daylight and temperature may trigger the molts.

Kōlea are unusual because they are one of the few native species whose living conditions have actually gotten better because of human activity. Since ancient times, people have cleared the land to make room for farms, homes, and other kinds of development. This has created more open, grassy areas where *kōlea* can hunt insects. Today, *kōlea* are plentiful and can be found almost anywhere where there is open grass: fields, pastures, salt marshes, mud flats, beaches, airports, cemeteries, sports fields, parks, playgrounds, golf courses, military bases, and people's lawns.

Sunbathing Turtles

SPECIES: Hawaiian green sea turtle
SCIENTIFIC NAME: *Chelonia mydas*
HAWAIIAN NAME: *Honu*
CATEGORY: Endemic Native Hawaiian Species
STATUS: Threatened

Hovering in the shallow water just offshore, a Hawaiian green sea turtle drifts back and forth with the tide, **browsing** on seaweed. After a while he turns and rides a wave toward the beach, then uses his front flippers to slowly push his body out of the water and onto the sand.

Other turtles already lie motionless on the beach, their brown shells dry and dusted with sand. Out of reach of the waves breaking gently just below them, the turtles lie perfectly still, eyes closed. They are **basking** on the sand.

Hawaiian green sea turtles, called *honu* by Hawaiians, are perfectly adapted for life in the sea but are heavy and awkward on land. Most species of sea turtle never leave the water except when females emerge to dig nests and lay eggs. Only some green sea turtles, second largest of the seven sea turtle species, come out of the ocean to bask.

Both male and female green sea turtles bask, youngsters as well as adults. Green sea turtles live in all the warmer oceans of the world, but only in Hawai'i, the **Galapagos Islands**, and remote parts of Australia do they bask. Of these three places, Hawai'i has the best basking areas and the largest number of turtles that come ashore.

Why do they do it? We know that green sea turtles are **cold-blooded**, and like all cold-blooded creatures, they need to get warmth and energy from sunshine in order for their bodies to work well. When a sea turtle lies in the sun on the beach, its top shell, or **carapace**, absorbs heat. This heat seeps through the shell to the turtle's lungs, which lie just below its carapace. From there, the turtle's bloodstream carries warmth to all parts of its body.

Scientists who study green sea turtles believe that basking helps them in other ways, too. Soaking in the sun helps their bodies absorb vitamin D, enables them to digest their food better, and uses up body fat. Also, the hot sun beating down on a turtle's carapace kills any **algae** growing there.

Female green sea turtles have special reasons to bask. They sometimes haul themselves out on the sand to keep males from bothering them during the mating season, and scientists think that basking helps their eggs develop more quickly.

Every once in a while, a basking turtle will sweep its front flippers back and toss sand onto its back. Sand on its shell keeps the turtle from getting *too* hot. If the sand is damp, it's cooling, and if the sand is dry, it deflects the sun's heat away from the turtle's body. The only other time a basking turtle moves is when it lifts its head to take a breath. The thick, salty tears that ooze from its eyes rid the turtle's body of extra salt and wash away the sand. Interestingly, basking turtles won't stay out in the rain. If it starts to rain, they push themselves back into the ocean.

In Hawai'i, *honu* often come ashore at night. Since there's no sun then to give heat, scientists think the turtles that haul out at night are trying to hold on to the heat they absorbed during the day. Or they may be trying to avoid predators, the big tiger sharks that prowl in shallow offshore waters.

Sometimes a sick *honu* will pull itself ashore. When this happens, the turtle is not basking. It has actually **stranded** itself. Scientists think that sick turtles do this to raise their body temperature and battle their illness.

In the past few years, more and more green sea turtles have come ashore to bask on the beaches of the main Hawaiian Islands. The turtles don't seem to mind people walking around them, but they are protected by law and can't be disturbed. On some beaches, volunteers stretch yellow warning tapes around basking turtles to keep people at a safe distance.

Only a few years ago, Hawaiian green sea turtles were in danger of becoming extinct. People used to catch and eat them or use their shells for tools and ornaments, and many turtles were drowned in fishing nets. Pollution or crowds of people using the beaches killed the sea grasses the turtles depend on for food, and plastics floating in the ocean got into their digestive systems and killed them. Today, because we know more about the green sea turtles and their life habits, and because we protect them, they are still threatened but no longer endangered.

Sea Spinners

SPECIES: Spinner dolphin
SCIENTIFIC NAME: *Stenella longirostris*
HAWAIIAN NAME: *Naiʻa*
CATEGORY: Indigenous Native Hawaiian Species
STATUS: Population numbers unknown

Early in the morning, spinner dolphins enter the shallow bay, many of them splashing and leaping as they come. The dolphins have chosen this bay with its white sandy bottom for their resting place because they can easily see any sharks or other predators that might lurk below. As the dolphins swim farther into the bay, they quiet down. They stop whistling and calling and swim more slowly, often touching or stroking each other with their fins or tail **flukes**. After a while, the whole **school** settles into a smooth, quiet rhythm, moving gracefully up and down together, almost as if they were one giant animal. The school is resting.

In the late afternoon, a dolphin pokes its nose out of the water. A minute later, another does the same. A third dolphin lifts its tail into the air and slaps the water. Rest time is over. The spinner dolphins are waking up. One dolphin leaps out of the water, spins in the air, and splashes down in a riot of bubbles. More dolphins leap and spin, gathering energy. The school swims in a zigzag pattern for a few moments, then, as the sun dips lower in the sky, heads out of the bay to feeding grounds in deeper offshore waters.

Spinners feed mostly at night and use **echolocation**, or sound, to scan the dark water for food. Spinners make sounds that bounce off objects and send echoes back, much like the sonar systems used by submarines. The dolphins "read" the echoes to find their prey. Spinners have more teeth than other dolphins, and they use them to munch on the small deep-ocean fish, shrimp, and squid that rise toward the surface of the ocean at night. The dolphins depend on their hearing to stay in contact in the dark, using clicks, whistles, bubble trails, and tail and fin slaps.

Spinner dolphins are found in warmer oceans all over the world, but they look different and act differently depending on where they live. All spinners have slim bodies, and all but one species has a long beak, or **rostrum**. Hawaiian spinners are beautifully colored, with a dark-gray back, light-gray sides, and a dark stripe that runs from eye to **pectoral** fin. Called *naiʻa* by the Hawaiians, spinner dolphins have been coming into Hawaiʻi's shallow bays since ancient times, long before humans arrived.

Other sea mammals can leap out of the water, but only spinner dolphins can spin their bodies in the air. They also have the amazing ability to throw themselves into the air and turn tail over head in a flying **somersault**. Scientists believe that when spinners spin, they aren't just playing but are doing something important to their survival. Some think they spin to get rid of parasites and remoras (fish that cling to the dolphins' skin), and others think the animals are communicating through their spinning leaps and loud splashes.

Spinners leap and spin more often during the night than during the day. Perhaps they are telling other dolphins where they are, or where the edges of the school are.

It's important that the dolphins stay in contact. Sometimes, they help each other round up fish. If danger threatens, the school tightens up for protection. Hawaiian spinners must stay on the alert for the large open-ocean predators that would harm them: tiger sharks, white-tipped sharks, cookie-cutter sharks, killer whales, and pilot whales.

Dolphins start to spin when they are still very young, practicing in the safety of shallow bays. People standing on the shore have seen baby dolphins jump again and again, trying to perfect their spins and tail slaps.

Human activity has threatened spinner dolphins: ocean pollution can make them sick, and they sometimes get caught in fishing nets and lines. Spinner dolphins are protected by the Marine Mammal Protection Act passed in 1972, which means it is against the law to hunt or bother them. Some people "love them too much" and want to swim or play with them. This may cause harm. If the dolphins are not able to get enough rest during the day, they may not have enough energy to hunt for food at night. When people try to get close to dolphins, they may interfere with mating activities or bother mother dolphins tending to their calves.

Spinner dolphins can be seen near all the major islands of Hawai'i. Although scientists don't know exactly how many dolphins live in Hawaiian waters, the Hawaiian spinners are not an endangered species.

Singers of the Deep

SPECIES: Humpback whale

SCIENTIFIC NAME: *Megaptera novaeangliae*

HAWAIIAN NAME: *Koholā*

CATEGORY: Indigenous Native Hawaiian Species

STATUS: Endangered

In winter, the whales come to Hawaiʻi. They swim through almost three thousand miles of open ocean from their feeding grounds off Alaska, Canada, and the northwest United States. They come to Hawaiʻi's shallow coastal waters to have their babies or find mates, and when they come, they sing.

The males are the singers. Female humpbacks have been recorded making sounds, but their sounds are not considered "songs." Usually, each male sings alone, but sometimes he may sing when traveling with another male or even, later in the season, with a female and her new calf.

When the male sings alone, he often gets into a special position: he rests head-down about 50–75 feet below the surface of the ocean, closes his eyes, and points his tail to the sky. He makes sets of sounds called "themes," which he repeats over and over as a song. Normally, a song lasts between six and eighteen minutes, but researchers in Hawaiʻi once stopped their boat and listened to a whale sing for fourteen hours, and when they left the area, he was still singing.

If you dropped a hydrophone, a special microphone for underwater sounds, into the water, you probably wouldn't call the whale noises a "song." To us, whale song sounds like loud groans, creaks, blasts, or shrieks. Many whale sounds are very low in tone, sometimes too low for humans to hear. Researchers have noticed that whale songs are somewhat like the "songs" of land-dwelling mammals, such as elephants.

All the male humpbacks in Hawai'i sing the same song, but as the winter weeks pass, the song changes. Singers may create new themes or alter old ones. Each singer adjusts his song so that he is singing the same song as all the other singers. By the end of March, when the whales begin to head back north, their song is different from the song they sang when they arrived in November. During the feeding season in the Arctic, the humpbacks either don't sing at all or don't sing very much, so their song doesn't change. The song the males sing during the next trip south is the same one they sang going north the previous spring.

Sometimes, humpbacks in other breeding grounds (near Japan, Mexico, or the Philippines) sing songs that are partly the same as the whale song in Hawai'i. How do the other whales learn these Hawai'i songs when they are so far away? Scientists think they either hear them during migration or pick up snatches of song in the feeding grounds, where whales from different breeding grounds mix together.

Why do whales sing? Researchers are trying to find out. They all agree that the songs are a form of communication. Humpback whales, both male and female, can make a variety of sounds. They use "social sounds" when traveling slowly or resting, especially mothers and their calves. They also have a "feeding call" they use in the northern feeding grounds. Whales depend on their sense of hearing rather than sight, because sound, especially **low-frequency** sound, carries a long way in water, and sight is limited. Sound travels five to six times faster in water than it does in air. Some scientists think that, many years ago, some whale sounds may have traveled as far as ten thousand miles! Today, shipping and other human activities have created so much noise in the underwater world of whales that sounds can't be heard very far away.

Humpback songs seem to be important to mating, because they are only sung fully during the winter breeding season. Perhaps the males are telling other whales where they are, or maybe they're trying to scare away competing males. Or they could be trying to attract a female or get other males to help them attract females. Sometimes, young males may just be practicing. One interesting idea is that the songs help female whales figure out which males are the strongest and healthiest. The females want to choose the best mates so that their future calves have the best chance of survival.

Humpback whales' major predators are killer whales and sharks that attack young or sick humpbacks. More threats come from human activity. Fishing nets or long lines left in the sea may entangle whales and keep them from rising to the surface to breathe, or the lines may cut into the whale's body. Sometimes ships bump into slow-swimming whales, causing injury or death. Because of the Endangered Species Act and the Marine Mammal Protection Act, it is against the law to bother or kill a humpback whale in United States waters. In 1992, the United States Congress established the Hawaiian Islands Humpback National Marine Sanctuary to protect humpback whales in their breeding territory.

Expert Climbers

SPECIES: Mountain shrimp

SCIENTIFIC NAME: *Atyoida bisulcata*

HAWAIIAN NAMES: *'Ōpae kala'ole, 'Ōpae kuahiwi, 'Ōpae kolo*

CATEGORY: Endemic Native Hawaiian Species

STATUS: Fairly plentiful in upper mountain streams on O'ahu, Hawai'i, Moloka'i, Maui, and Kaua'i

When a repairman was fixing an air conditioner on the roof of a building in Honolulu, he looked down and could hardly believe his eyes. A group of little shrimp was gathered under the drip pan! How in the world, he wondered, could shrimp get to the top of a five-story building? A marine scientist told the repairman that the shrimp must have come from a nearby stream. They had somehow gotten into a storm drain and then climbed up the building's drainpipe to the roof. What the repairman had discovered were young *'ōpae kala'ole,* Hawai'i's astonishing climbing shrimp.

Only two inches long, adult *'ōpae kala'ole* are usually found in swift-moving streams high in the mountains, picking their way among the rocks and boulders. In the clear, flowing water of the upland mountain streams, the shrimp look for food, grow, and mate.

'Ōpae kala'ole have a complicated life cycle. They are **diadromous**, which means they spend part of their life in the ocean and the rest of their life in freshwater. Female shrimp can lay eggs when they are one year old, and they carry their eggs attached to their legs, or **swimmerets**. Each female can carry over three thousand eggs at one time! Two months after they are laid in freshwater streams, the eggs are ready to hatch. *'Ōpae kala'ole* eggs don't hatch into **larvae** until rainfall pours into the mountain streams and causes large amounts of water to crash and tumble along the rocks. Then the tiny brown larvae are carried by the fast-flowing currents down the mountain and out into the sea. In the ocean, they drift with the **plankton** for two months, molting (shedding their skin) and growing before they return to the stream as young shrimp.

When they are less than one-fourth of an inch long, the young shrimp leave the ocean and return to the freshwater streams. Using their tiny pointed legs and bristly leg hairs, the little shrimp move up the rushing mountain streams, often using mosses and ferns as "ladders" to climb upward. The little shrimp plunge headfirst into the flowing current, climbing over rocks and walls, traveling through tunnels and pipes, and picking their way up steep waterfalls. They have been known to climb through crashing waterfalls more than 1,400 feet high! The climbing instinct is very strong. If water is poured down the side of a bucket with young shrimp inside, the little 'ōpae will try to climb up the stream of water.

Once they reach the upper parts of the mountain streams, the young shrimp settle down. When stream water moves slowly, they crawl among the rocks, using their tiny pincers to pick bits of food from the stream bottom. When the water moves swiftly, the shrimp face into the current and spread the tiny hairs on their front legs. The hairs work like catchers' mitts, trapping food particles, which the 'ōpae shove into their mouths. Sometimes, many shrimp line up side by side across the stream and stand with their front legs outstretched.

Hawaiians had many names for these climbing shrimp, including *ʻōpae kalaʻole* (spineless shrimp), *ʻōpae kuahiwi* (mountain shrimp), and *ʻōpae kolo* (crawling shrimp). They were a favorite food in old Hawaiʻi.

Mountain shrimp are still gathered for food today, but because most of Hawaiʻi's streams have been changed, the animals are not as plentiful as in days of old. In modern Hawaiʻi, many streams have been channelized, which means they have been directed into concrete pathways to provide water to farms instead of flowing naturally out to sea. Making streams flow into channels helped people develop the land for farms, houses, and businesses, but it destroyed the habitats of many stream creatures. *ʻŌpae kalaʻole* are not yet an endangered species, and scientists are looking for ways to protect their stream habitats from further destruction.

Killer Caterpillars

SPECIES: Carnivorous caterpillar
SCIENTIFIC NAME: *Eupithecia*
HAWAIIAN NAME: *'Enuhe hamui'a*
CATEGORY: Endemic Native Hawaiian Species
STATUS: Uncommon, endangered

Sitting on the edge of a green leaf, its head slightly lifted in the air, the small inchworm looks harmless. A fly crawling along the leaf brushes against tiny hairs on the tail end of the inchworm and, faster than you can snap your fingers, the inchworm bends backward, grabs the fly in his short, clawed arms, whips back around, and begins to eat it.

The innocent-looking inchworm is actually a killer caterpillar, one of six named species of caterpillar living in Hawai'i that are not found anywhere else in the world.

Some people call these caterpillars "inchworms" or "measuring worms" because of the way they crawl. They have no legs in the center part of their body. They move by creeping forward with their back legs and humping their backs until the back legs are just behind the front legs, then sliding the front part of their body forward. It looks like they are measuring the leaf or branch they're moving on.

These caterpillars are the young, or larvae, of a common family of moths, *Eupithecia*, which are found all over the world. But only in Hawai'i have these larvae become **carnivores**. In other parts of the world they feed on plants. For many years, no one realized that the Hawaiian caterpillars were insect eaters. Specimens that were captured always died in laboratories because scientists fed them plant matter, thinking the caterpillars were plant eaters. One day, a fly landed in a cage with a captive caterpillar, and when the scientists saw the caterpillar eat the fly, they realized they had been wrong. On examining the caterpillar more closely, they saw that it had claws for grabbing prey and long thin "trigger" hairs on the back end of its abdomen.

Hawai'i's *Eupithecia* inchworms eat many different kinds of insects: flies, ants, wasps, crickets, cockroaches, and moths. If an insect touches the caterpillar's front end, the caterpillar doesn't seem to mind, but the hairs (called **setae**) on their tail ends are sensitive to an insect's touch. When the caterpillar feels something brush against these setae, it spins its upper body around and uses its front legs to grab the insect. The caterpillar's sharp claws punch through the hard outer skeleton of the captured insect and hold it helpless while the caterpillar munches away.

Altogether, Hawai'i has twenty-two species of carnivorous, or insect-eating, caterpillars, all of the same moth family. The caterpillars eat insects at every stage of their development, starting with tiny insects like lice when the larvae are small, and, as they grow bigger, larger insects like flies or mosquitoes.

Inchworms are very well camouflaged. Their green or brown colors match their backgrounds exactly, making them very hard to see. Some inchworms stand with their front ends lifted up, looking exactly like little twigs. Others lie along the edges or stems of leaves and look like part of the leaf.

Most carnivorous caterpillars are "sit-and-wait" predators and will hold still for long periods of time, waiting for food to come near them. They are very patient and may stay in the same place for days or weeks. One species doesn't sit and wait but crawls along leaves looking for **galls**, places where small insects have burrowed into the leaf. When the caterpillar finds the galls, he eats the insects inside.

Scientists believe that the killer caterpillars, commonly called "grappling inchworms," turned into predators after they arrived in the Hawaiian islands, millions of years before humans came. The moths must have been blown over vast distances of ocean and, when they landed, found themselves in a place where there were no predators and very few other insects to compete with for food.

Over millions of years, the caterpillars changed. Scientists think that two things about the caterpillars helped them evolve into insect eaters: they already ate protein-rich flower pollen, and they had a defense behavior of snapping. Because ancient Hawai'i had no predator insects like praying mantids or ambush bugs, there was a niche in the environment the caterpillars could fill. As they slowly evolved into insect eaters, the caterpillars also diversified, which means they spread out and adapted to different living areas.

Hawai'i's carnivorous caterpillars were unknown until the 1970s, when their special adaptations were first observed. In 2005, another type of carnivorous caterpillar, one that spins webs and feeds on snails, was discovered. This recent discovery makes us wonder what other fascinating insect species may be hidden in Hawai'i's unexplored forests.

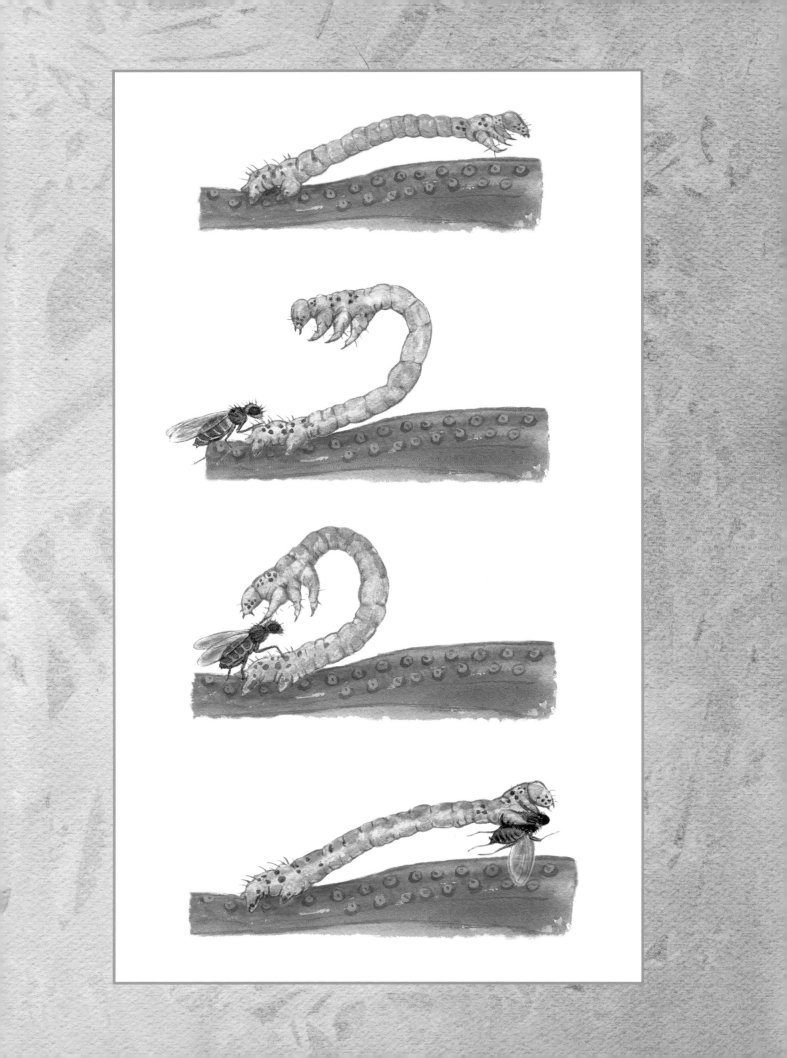

Vampire Bugs

SPECIES: Wēkiu

SCIENTIFIC NAME: *Nysius wekiuicola*

HAWAIIAN NAME: *Wēkiu*

CATEGORY: Endemic Native Hawaiian Species

STATUS: Not endangered

On the **summit** of Mauna Kea, the air is thin, wind whips across the rocky surface, and the temperature can drop ninety degrees between day and night. Snow covers the ground in winter, and only a few inches below the rocky surface the earth is frozen solid. Few plants and animals can survive in this harsh, dry habitat, but it is home to one of the most unusual insects in the world, the *wēkiu* bug.

For a long time, people thought nothing lived on the **barren** mountaintop. Mauna Kea is the tallest mountain on earth, rising 30,600 feet from its base at the bottom of the sea. The summit is like an island, separated from other ecosystems by its high elevation. The land looks empty; its tough grasses, mosses, and other plants are sparse and scattered. It wasn't until 1979 that scientists turning over rocks discovered the *wēkiu* bug. Named for the cinder cone that forms the very top of Mauna Kea, the *wēkiu* belongs to a family of seed-eating insects that are common in Hawai'i. These insects have strong tube-like mouthparts that they poke through the tough skins of seeds to suck out the soft insides.

Since there are no seeds on the top of Mauna Kea, the scientists wondered what the *wēkiu* was eating. They discovered that the bug had turned into a predator: it had somehow figured out how to use its mouth parts to pierce the bodies of dead and dying insects and, like a vampire, suck out their body juices.

Insects that live on the lower, warmer parts of Mauna Kea can't survive the winds and cold dry air of the summit. When they have the bad luck to be blown to the top, they become **moribund**, or inactive, and soon they die. Sometimes, flies and ladybugs fly to the summit to mate, not realizing that the cold will kill them. *Wēkiu* bugs scramble through the rocks and cinders on their long legs to find dead and dying insects, and when there is snow on the ground, they gather at the edges of the melting snow to look for insect bodies that may have been trapped inside.

Why don't *wēkiu* bugs freeze like the other insects? Scientists used to think the *wēkiu* had a kind of **antifreeze** in their blood that kept them alive in the cold weather. Now they know that the bugs' dark body color absorbs warmth from the sun and enables them to spend short periods of time above ground. The bugs also keep themselves warm by going underground and finding warmer places in between the cinders. *Wēkiu* bugs are very small, less than one-fourth of an inch long, so they can easily find shelter. They don't have fully formed wings and can't fly, which probably keeps them from getting blown into space.

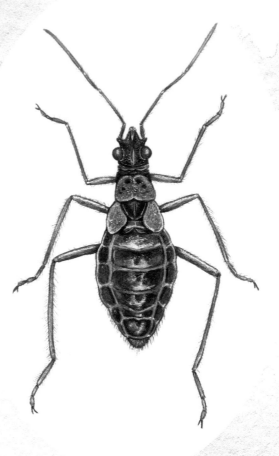

Wēkiu bugs are found nowhere else in the world. They share their high-altitude habitat with a handful of other small native insects: mites, spiders, a centipede as big as your eyelash, and a three-fourths-of-an-inch-long wolf spider that lies in ambush under rocks and preys on any moving insect, including the *wēkiu*.

A few years ago, there seemed to be fewer *wēkiu* bugs on Mauna Kea's summit, and scientists worried that human activity was putting them in danger. The thin, clear air and lack of lights from cities or towns make Mauna Kea an excellent location for the giant telescopes that allow us to peer into outer space. Building and using these telescopes has caused some damage to the fragile cinder-cone environment. In addition, hikers and motor vehicles create dust, which can clog the spaces between cinders where the tiny *wēkiu* moves. The scientists also considered that natural causes might be responsible for the drop in numbers. They wondered if less snowfall in recent years had affected the *wēkiu* or if newly introduced insect species were preying on them.

Scientists now realize the *wēkiu* are not disappearing. There are simply times when plenty of the little bugs can be found and times when they are scarce. Although they don't yet know why the numbers change, researchers have become better at finding and trapping the insects, so they are also better at figuring out how many there are. Scientists continue to study the *wēkiu* to learn more about how this unusual insect manages to survive in Mauna Kea's harsh environment.

Flying Acrobats

SPECIES: Hawaiian bat
SCIENTIFIC NAME: *Lasiurus cinereus semotus*
HAWAIIAN NAME: *ʻŌpeʻapeʻa*
CATEGORY: Endemic Native Hawaiian Species
STATUS: Endangered

A brisk evening breeze blows down the mountains on the Big Island of Hawaiʻi, picking up insects and blowing them out over the ocean, where they hover over the waves. Just before sunset, a small bat flies out of the shoreline forest and heads down the river to the sea. Another bat appears, then another, until there are five bats flying straight out to sea. When they reach the cloud of insects blown out by the wind, they stop their headlong flight and become acrobats in the sky, soaring and darting and diving, sometimes even turning flips in the air. The bats are catching their dinner.

The Hawaiian hoary bat, called *ʻōpeʻapeʻa* by the Hawaiians, is an **insectivore**. Its jaws are strong enough to crunch hard beetle shells. Compared to mainland bats, the Hawaiian bat is not a picky eater. It will eat flies, small wasps, grasshoppers, dragonflies, and even pests such as sugarcane leafhoppers and termites. When Hawaiian bats catch moths in the air, they zoom in from behind and bite off the moth's soft body, letting the legs and wings drop to the ground. Sometimes a bat will use its hand-like wing to swat an insect into its tail pouch. When the bat ducks its head downward to grab the insect, it flips tail-over-head in the air, just like a circus acrobat doing a somersault.

Flying takes a huge amount of energy, so bats have to eat a lot. A hoary bat can eat up to 40 percent of its body weight in a single meal. That's like an eighty-pound person eating thirty-two pounds of food for dinner! The bats digest their food very quickly; it takes only

twenty minutes for food to go through their digestive systems. Sometimes, bats chew and swallow their food while they fly. Other times, they take food back to their roosts to eat.

Hawaiian bats are shy, solitary creatures that live on the islands of Hawai'i, Kaua'i, and perhaps Maui. They are called "hoary" bats because their fur is tipped with white, making them look like they were dipped in hoarfrost. They belong to the biggest of all bat families, the evening bats.

Scientists think Hawaiian bats may be the rarest bats in the world. Because bats are the only mammals that can fly, they were the only land mammals to find their way to Hawai'i, probably blown off course during a storm. No one knows how many bats are in Hawai'i because they are very hard to catch and study. They are active only at dusk or in the dark, and the color of their fur is excellent camouflage, making them almost invisible when they roost in trees.

When they hunt in the dark, Hawaiian bats use echolocation to find their prey. As they fly, they send out high-pitched sounds (higher than humans can hear), which bounce off objects and go back to the bats as echoes. By "reading" the echoes, the bats can figure out the size and shape of the object and figure out how it moves. Moths try to escape the bats by dropping to the ground or flying into trees and bushes. The Hawaiian bats are excellent fliers, fast and **agile**, and they will chase moths to within inches of the ground.

Hawaiian bats don't have many natural predators. Hawks and owls may chase them in the air, and sometimes rats and feral cats will climb up trees to prey on baby bats. On occasion, young bats that can't fly very well get caught in barbed-wire fences, and very rarely, a car hits one.

Humans are the bats' worst enemy. Hawaiian bats roost in trees, so when humans cut down trees to clear land for farms or towns, they destroy bat habitats. Humans use deadly chemicals and pesticides that are poisonous to bats, and they build huge windmills that kill and injure them.

People are afraid of bats, probably because they've heard scary stories about them. Most people don't realize how helpful bats are; they think they are just are weird-looking creatures that fly in the dark and have sharp teeth. The truth is that these little flying acrobats help us by killing millions of insect pests each year. Without realizing it, humans may be speeding up the extinction of one of Hawaiʻi's most graceful and helpful creatures.

Glossary and Pronunciation Guide

agile (A-jil)—able to move quickly and easily

algae (AL-jee)—simple, plant-like organisms that grow in sunlit waters. Seaweed is a form of algae.

alien (AY-lee-en)—a plant or animal living in an area where it is not native or indigenous

antifreeze—a chemical that keeps a liquid from freezing

archipelago (ar-kih-PEL-ih-go)—a group of islands

atoll (AT-tole)—a coral island shaped like a ring

barren—without plants, bare

basking—lying in a bright, warm place

boobies—tropical seabirds, often with brightly colored feet

botulism (BAH-chu-liz-em)—poisoning caused by eating food containing certain bacteria

browsing—eating leaves or plants

camouflage (KAM-o-flaj)—the color and sometimes the behavior of an animal that enables it to blend into its surroundings

carapace (KAH-ra-pase)—the upper shell of a turtle

carnivore (KAR-nih-vor)—an animal that feeds on other animals, a meat eater

centipede (SEN-tih-peed)—an insect-like creature with a flattened body that is divided into segments. Each segment has a pair of legs, except for the first, which has a pair of poison fangs.

chemical defenses—poison, bitter taste, or other harmful or unpleasant taste or smell produced by a plant or animal to ward off predators

cold-blooded—having a body temperature that is the same as the temperature of the surrounding air or water

compete—to try to be more successful than others

contaminate—to make something dangerous or impure by adding something to it

diadromous (dye-AD-druh-mus)—to migrate between fresh and salt water

disruptive coloration—color patterns that hide or blur the shape of an animal's body, making it hard to see

echolocation (ek-o-lo-KAY-shun)—the use of sounds and echoes to locate objects

ecosystem (EE-ko-sis-tem)—the interaction of all living and nonliving things that exist together in a certain area. All things within an ecosystem are dependent on each other for survival.

endemic (en-DEM-ik)—belonging to a particular location

Eupithecia **(you-pih-THEE-see-a)**—a common type of moth found all over the world

evolution—a theory that today's plants and animals are descended from other kinds of plants and animals that lived long ago, and that the plants and animals inherited differences and passed them down through many generations

evolved—changed, usually from a simpler to a more complex form

extinct—no longer existing. For example, dinosaurs are extinct.

feral (FAIR-ul)—an animal that used to be tame and is now wild

flukes—the two large sides of a whale or dolphin's tail

Galapagos (gah-LAH-pah-goz) Islands—a group of small islands that lie across the equator 575 miles off the west coast of Ecuador in South America

galls—growths, caused by insects or fungus, found on the leaves, stems, or roots of plants

hatchlings—young that have just come out of their eggs

indigenous (in-DIJ-ih-nus)—living in a certain area

inflate—blow up, expand

insectivore (in-SEK-tih-vor)—an animal that eats insects

Kīlauea (kee-laoo-WAY-ah)—a volcano on the southeastern side of the island of Hawai'i. Kīlauea is the most active volcano on earth.

koi (KOY)—a kind of fish (carp) that is bred for its large size and bright colors

larvae (LAR-vee)—newly hatched or born offspring of animals without backbones. Larvae change their forms (metamorphose) as they grow into their adult stage.

lava—molten (melted) rock from a volcano, or molten rock that has cooled and hardened

low frequency—very deep, low sounds, sometimes too low for humans to hear

magma—hot liquid rock below the surface of the earth

millipede (MIL-ih-peed)—an insect-like creature with a long, thin body and many legs

molt—to lose hair, horns, outer skin, or feathers and grow replacements

moribund (MOR-ih-bund)—no longer active, close to death

niche (nitch)—the specific place of an organism within its habitat

parasite—an animal that lives in or on another animal and gets food or protection from it

pectoral (PEK-tor-ul) fins—fins on a fish or marine mammal that are located in the chest area, like the front legs of a land mammal

plankton—very small plant and animal life found in oceans, lakes, and other bodies of water

plumage (PLOOM-ij)—feathers that cover the body of a bird

preen—to straighten or clean feathers with the beak

progenitors (pro-JEN-ih-torz)—ancestors; animals in the past that are related to today's animals

resident—one who lives in a certain place

rostrum (RAH-strum)—the beak or snout of a dolphin

sanctuaries (SANK-chu-air-ees)—a place where animals and/or plants are protected

school—a group of fish, usually of the same species and age or size, that swim together in an organized manner

seamount—an underwater mountain that does not reach the surface of the sea

setae (SEE-tee)—stiff hairs

somersault (SUM-mer-salt)—an acrobatic motion where the body revolves in a full circle with the feet passing over the head

strand—to become "beached" or stuck in shallow water

summit—the highest point

swimmerets—small leg-like structures on each side of a shrimp's abdomen that help with swimming and, in the female, hold eggs in place

tectonic (tek-TOHN-ik) plates—the giant pieces that cover the earth's surface like a jigsaw puzzle. Tectonic plates are in constant, but very slow, motion.

toxic—containing poison

water hyacinth (HI-ah-sinth)—an invasive floating plant that can grow in thick layers covering the surface of lakes or streams

wēkiu **(VAY-kee-you)**—an insect that lives only on the summit of Mauna Kea

wetlands—land areas that are saturated with water; marshes, swamps

To Learn More

Ching, Patrick. *Sea Turtles of Hawai'i*. Honolulu: University of Hawai'i Press, 2001.

Coste, Marion. *The Hawaiian Bat 'Ōpe'ape'a*. Honolulu: University of Hawai'i Press, 2005.

———. *Honu*. Honolulu: University of Hawai'i Press, 1993.

———. *Kōlea:The Story of the Pacific Golden Plover*. Honolulu: University of Hawai'i Press, 1998.

Furgang, Kathy. *Kilauea: Hawaii's Most Active Volcano*. New York: Powerkids Press, 2003.

Gentle, Victor, and Janet Perry. *Humpback Whales*. Milwaukee: Gareth Stevens Publishing, 2001.

Miller, Debbie S. *Flight of the Golden Plover: The Amazing Migration between Hawaii and Alaska*. Portland, OR: Alaska Northwest Books, 1996.

Mira, Monika. *Hawaii's Green Sea Turtles* (Science and Nature for Young Readers). Kindle edition, Amazon Digital Services Inc., 2012.

Orr, Katherine Shelley. *Discover Hawaii Freshwater Wildlife*. Honolulu: Island Heritage Publishing, 1997.

Orr, Katherine S. *Discover Hawaii's Marine Mammals*. Honolulu: Island Heritage Publishing, 1998.

Orr, Katherine, and Mauliola Cook. *Discover Hawaii's Volcanoes: Birth by Fire*. Honolulu: Island Heritage Publishing, 2010.

Patent, Dorothy Hinshaw. *Humpback Whales*. New York: Holiday House, 1989.

Prevost, John. *Spinner Dolphins*. Edina, MN: Abdo and Daughters, 1996.

Scott, Susan. *Plants and Animals of Hawaii*. Honolulu: Bess Press, 1991.

Webster, Christine. *The Magic Schoolbus Blows Its Top: A Book about Volcanoes*. New York: Scholastic Inc., 1996.

———. *Mauna Loa: The Largest Volcano in the United States* (Natural Wonders Series). New York: Weigl Publishers, 2004.

Acknowledgments

Thank you to the following people who generously shared their time and expertise to help with the development of this book: Allen Allison, senior zoologist, Bishop Museum; Amy Bickham Baird, assistant professor of biology, Department of Natural Sciences, University of Houston–Downtown; George Balazs, zoologist, team leader, Marine Turtle Research Program, Pacific Islands Fisheries Science Center; Neal L. Evenhuis, senior entomologist, Bishop Museum; Molly Hagemann, vertebrate zoology collections manager, Bishop Museum; Emmanuelle Martinez, senior research scientist, Pacific Whale Foundation; Catherine Ortenberger, natural history educator; Thane K. Pratt, wildlife biologist, Bishop Museum research affiliate; Julian Tyne, PhD candidate, Murdoch University Cetacean Research Unit, Perth, Western Australia; and Eric VanderWerf, wildlife biologist, co-owner of Pacific Conservation Rim.

About the Author

MARION COSTE, a graduate of Connecticut College, has been involved in the field of education for more than forty years as an elementary schoolteacher, college instructor, teacher trainer, and museum director. Growing up on the New Jersey shore Marion loved to learn about how different animals live in the wild. She was introduced to the fascinating and fragile world of native Hawaiian wildlife by researchers and colleagues at Bishop Museum in Honolulu. Coste is the author of four other books about Hawaiian native species: *Nēnē* (Hawaiian goose), *Honu* (Hawaiian green sea turtle), *Kōlea* (Pacific golden plover), and the Hawaiian bat, *ʻŌpeʻapeʻa*. She has also written *Wild Beach,* a book about a barrier island beach off Charleston, South Carolina, and *Finding Joy,* the story of a family who adopted a baby girl from China. She was awarded the Anna Cross Giblin nonfiction grant from the Society of Children's Book Writers and Illustrators in 1991, received the 1999 *Ka Palapala Poʻokela* Award for excellence in children's literature for *Kōlea,* and honorable mention for the same award in 2006 for *The Hawaiian Bat.*

About the Illustrator

RENA EKMANIS is a natural science illustrator and fine artist dedicated to conservation, environmental awareness, and environmental education through art. She has a BFA in drawing from California College of the Arts, a Science Illustration Graduate Certificate from California State University, Monterey Bay, and a Montessori Teaching Certificate from Montessori Education Center of the Rockies. Rena works in a variety of mediums including watercolor, acrylics, oil paints, ceramic sculpture, and digital media. Among her favorite subjects are cetaceans and other marine life, birds, and endangered species. The artist loves to spend time in the field, hiking, swimming, and scuba diving, in order to get close to her subjects and observe them in their natural habitats. Rena hopes that her artwork contributes to a greater awareness of the miraculous flora and fauna of the earth. She lives on the Big Island of Hawaiʻi.